P9-CCD-573

Copyright © 2010
Brownlow
6309 Airport Freeway
Fort Worth, Texas 76117

All rights reserved. The use or
reprinting of any part of this book
without written permission of the
publisher is prohibited.

ISBN 978-1-59177-919-3

Printed in China

STORIES FROM THE OLD
AND NEW TESTAMENTS

First published in 1851

Edited by Paul C. Brownlow

CONTENTS

Foreword

Contents

FOREWORD

In 1851, an obscure publisher printed and bound a miniature Bible for children. In reality, it was a Bible storybook, but the beautiful leather cover carried the word, "Bible."

We have endeavored to reproduce the original text of the 1851 edition and combine it with charming illustrations from various nineteenth-century children's Bible storybooks. This new edition is designed to be a beautiful "first Bible" and keepsake for every new baby.

⌒∞⌒

1: THE FIRST FAMILY

In the beginning, God created the heavens and the earth, with every plant and living thing. He also brought into being the sun, the moon and stars, and placed them in the heavens. And last of all he made a man, named Adam, and a woman, whose name was Eve. He put them in a garden where it was so warm that they did not need a house. The beasts were playful and tame, and plenty of fruit hung upon the trees.

There was only one tree of which God said they should not eat. Yet they partook of the fruit of that very tree!

Until then they were happy, but they soon became miserable. God called to them saying they had done evil; and although they tried to hide, he found them hiding in the thickest shade.

God's angel drove them out of their once happy garden, to wander and to labor on the earth for their food. God said they would have to work hard for their food until they died and returned to the ground, out of which they were taken.

After Adam and Eve were driven from the pleasant garden of Eden, they had two sons, Cain and Abel. The first was of an angry disposition, and hated his brother because Abel was meek. Although God reasoned with Cain, his anger and hatred grew so strong against Abel, that he killed him.

And the Lord said unto Cain, "Where is Abel your brother?" And Cain said, "I do not know. Am I my brother's keeper?" God knew what Cain had done and sentenced him to be a fugitive and vagabond on the earth forever.

Adam and Eve, having disobeyed their Maker, and Cain having killed his brother, their children and children's children became at last very wicked. God determined to punish them by a flood of water, which would drown all but Noah and his family.

While others turned away from serving God, Noah did not forget to worship and obey God. He was a just man, and perfect in his generation because Noah walked with God. And the Lord not only gave warning to the righteous Noah of what he was about to do,

but directed him how to make an ark. The large boat, or ark, would preserve Noah, his family and two of every kind of beast, bird and creeping thing that lived in the air or on the earth.

Noah was six hundred years old when he entered into the ark. And the Lord caused a great and terrible rain of forty days and forty nights to fall on the earth. The fountains of the great deep were broken up, and the windows of heaven were opened, and all the high hills and mountains were covered with water. All creatures on the face of the earth were destroyed, except Noah and those with him in the ark.

And God made a wind to pass over the earth, and the waters receded. At God's command, Noah went out of the ark and brought every living thing with him. And the animals again spread on the earth and increased abundantly.

Remembering God, Noah built an altar and offered sacrifices to the Lord. God said, "I will not again curse the ground for man's sake. Neither shall the earth be destroyed any more by the waters of a flood." And God placed a rainbow in the cloud, in token of the covenant between him and the earth.

3: ABRAHAM, THE FRIEND OF GOD

In due time, Abraham was called by God to be the father of the Jewish nation and of all the truly faithful. Abraham obeyed God's command to leave his home, and to follow God as a pilgrim and sojourner. He lived in tents, and God spoke to him often. Abraham was thus a faithful servant and he became the friend of God.

When Abraham was a hundred years old, God sent him and his wife, Sarah, a son – the promised son of their old age. His name was Isaac. Now Abraham loved Isaac very much, but he loved God still more as shown by his obedience to God's command.

When God called Abraham to offer his son for a sacrifice, Abraham made preparations to accomplish it. He and Isaac and the servants journeyed three days to the place God had told Abraham to go.

Having built an altar and laid on the wood, he bound his son and laid him on the altar. Just as he raised the knife to slay his child, an angel called to Abraham to halt.

Looking round, Abraham found a ram with his horns entangled in a thicket. Abraham went and took the ram, and

offered him for a sacrifice, instead of his beloved son.

Abraham and Isaac returned home with thankful hearts rejoicing. God previously knew the depth of Abraham's faith, but now even Abraham knew the extent of his love, for he loved God more than his own flesh and blood.

Isaac learned to love God from his father, and Isaac served God faithfully. As Isaac grew up, he used to go into the fields in the early evening to meditate on the wisdom and goodness of his Maker.

ow Isaac had two sons, Esau the elder, and Jacob the younger. In those days it was considered a privilege to be firstborn. But Esau, being weak with hunger, sold his birthright to Jacob for a mess of pottage.

When it came time for Isaac to bless his firstborn son, Isaac's wife, Rebekah, plotted to deceive him. She gave instructions to Jacob to put on the garments of Esau so that he would smell like Esau. She further gave him instructions to cover his arms and hands and neck with goat skins so that he would feel hairy like his brother.

Then she made a savory meal for Jacob to serve Isaac.

Isaac, being old and his eyes dim, could not see that Jacob brought the meal and received the blessing for the firstborn, instead of Esau. When Esau came into the tent of Isaac to be blessed, he cried with an exceeding and great cry when he realized the blessing was given to Jacob. And Esau hated Jacob because of the blessing and made schemes to kill him.

Therefore, Jacob went into a far country to escape from Esau and to take a wife.

5: JOSEPH AND HIS BRETHREN

God blessed Jacob and increased his flocks and his herds and his wealth. And Jacob married Leah and Rachel, and in due time, he had twelve sons.

Now, Jacob loved Joseph more than his other sons. Joseph was given a special coat of many colors, and his brothers hated him all the more. In his simplicity and innocence, Joseph told his brothers some remarkable dreams he had. Their hatred increased so much that they sold him, and he was carried to Egypt as a slave.

Potiphar, an officer of Pharaoh, purchased Joseph and made him ruler over all his house. When Potiphar's wife made immodest requests of him, Joseph ignored her. In haste and in revenge, she accused him falsely to his master who cast him into prison.

When Joseph was thirty years old, he was brought from prison to interpret the dreams of Pharaoh. Joseph, by God's power, interpreted the dreams to mean that seven years of good crops would be followed by seven years of famine. As a result, Joseph was made governor of Egypt and by his counsel, the miseries of famine were prevented.

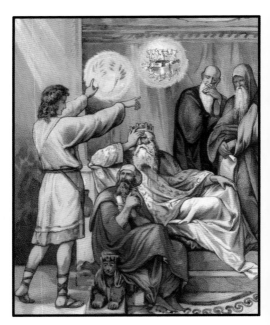

In due season, Joseph's brethren came to Egypt to buy corn, and bowed down to him, for they did not know him.

He seized them as spies, confined them in prison, and kept Simeon in Egypt until they brought Benjamin, his youngest brother. Upon seeing Benjamin, Joseph wept aloud and declared he was their brother whom they had sold. And with much tenderness, Joseph hugged Benjamin and embraced him.

Jacob, being told of Joseph's prosperity, went with all his family to Egypt. They settled in the fertile plains of Goshen where Jacob died in peace.

6: THE STORY OF MOSES

Now the children of Israel increased greatly in Egypt, where they were held in bondage. The Egyptians feared the Israelites, lest they should be the most powerful. Therefore the king of Egypt ordered that each male infant among the Israelites should be killed when born.

A certain Hebrew woman had a son, and fearing the king's decree, she kept him hid for three months. Finding she could no longer keep him secret, she prepared an ark, or cradle, of bulrushes. She coated it with mud and pitch, and put the child in it along the river's brink.

When Pharaoh's daughter went down to the river to bathe, she discovered the ark. Having compassion on the child, she took him and said, "This is one of the Hebrew's children." She found a nurse for the child which, unknown to her, was the child's real mother.

The child grew and was called the son of Pharaoh's daughter. And it came to pass when Moses was grown, he killed an Egyptian and hid the body in the sand. When Pharaoh heard this, he sought to kill Moses, and Moses fled and moved to Midian. Moses was directed to return to Egypt, and to tell Pharaoh, "Let my people go." God, by the hand of Moses, delivered the children of Israel from

their taskmasters in Egypt, according to his promise to Abraham.

Many plagues were inflicted on the Egyptians for their cruelty to the Israelites. On the evening before their departure, God passed over all the houses of the Israelites, and spared their firstborn. But those of the Egyptians were destroyed. And while the Israelites passed safely through the Red Sea on dry ground, Pharaoh and all his chariots and horsemen were drowned.

7: THE PROMISED LAND

Forty years the children of Israel journeyed in the wilderness, from the land of Egypt to Canaan. They were miraculously led by a pillar of cloud by day, and of fire by night. And they were fed with manna, a peculiar kind of food sent by God for them.

They had many enemies and difficulties to encounter, and they suffered much for their sins and disobedience. But in all their trials, they had a sure refuge of safety, when in sincerity of heart, they humbled themselves before the Lord, who led them out of four hundred years of forced bondage.

In the last year of travel of the children of Israel through the wilderness, Moses and his brother Aaron died. And Joshua succeeded Moses as God's chosen leader. On the appointed day, when the forty years had ended, the Lord miraculously divided the river Jordan, as he had done the Red Sea before for his chosen prophet. And the people passed over on dry ground.

Joshua led the people as they conquered many kings and powerful nations. He divided the land among the children of Israel and, having governed faithfully for twenty-four years, he died.

After the death of Joshua, the Israelites were governed by a number of judges and rulers. One such ruler was Samson, who was said to be the strongest of all men. When he was attacked by a lion, Samson caught him in his hands and killed the lion. At different times he slew many Philistines, and at one time he destroyed a thousand Philistines with a jawbone.

At his death, he killed more of them than he had in life by pulling down a house upon himself and those gathered therein.

8: LITTLE BOY SAMUEL

Now there was a man named Elkanah who had two wives, one with children and one with none. Hannah had no children, and year after year she went up to the house of Jehovah God and wept.

In sorrow, she wept and prayed, and she made a vow saying, "O Jehovah of hosts, if thou will look on my affliction and give unto me a son, then I will give him unto Jehovah all the days of his life."

And it came to pass that Hannah conceived, and gave birth to a son. She had

called his name Samuel. When she had weaned him, she took him with her to the house of God, and presented him to Eli, the high priest. And she worshipped the Lord and praised him greatly. But the child Samuel stayed with Eli, and served Jehovah in the temple.

One night when Samuel, while yet a child, was lying upon his bed, he heard a voice calling him by name. And he ran to Eli and said, "Here am I, for thou called me." But Eli had not called the child, and told him to lie down again.

This happened a second time, and Eli again instructed the child to lie down.

Upon the third time, Eli realized that Jehovah had called the child. Therefore, Eli told Samuel to go back, and next time he heard the voice to say, "Speak Lord, for thy servant listens." And God spoke to Samuel and told him of the

terrible curse that would soon fall on the sons of Eli because of their sinful ways.

And Samuel grew, and Jehovah was with him, and all Israel, from Dan to Beersheba, knew that Samuel was the prophet of God.

9 : DAVID, GOD'S ANOINTED

After a time the Israelites desired a king, and Saul was appointed. But while he was at war with the Philistines, Goliath the great giant defied the armies of Israel. Morning and evening for forty days, Goliath presented himself for battle, but no Israelite dared to meet him.

Though only a young shepherd, David heard of the giant and said, "Who is this Philistine that he should defy the armies of God? Jehovah, who delivered me out of the paw of the lion and of the bear, will deliver me out of the hand of this Philistine."

Going not in his own strength, but in the strength of the Lord, David took five smooth stones out of the brook and put them in his shepherd's bag. When Goliath looked about and saw that David was but a youth, he said, "Am I a dog that you come to me with staves?" And the Philistine cursed David.

David answered and said, "You come to me with a sword, and with a spear, and with a javelin, but I come to you in the name of Jehovah of hosts, the God of Israel." He then took a stone out of the bag and put it in a sling and struck the Philistine in his forehead. Then

David ran over to the giant, and took his sword and slew him, and cut off his head. When the Philistines saw that their champion was dead, they fled in much fear.

All the people praised David more than Saul, and Saul's anger burned against David. Saul even tried to kill David, the hero. Later, when Saul and his sons were dead, David was thirty years old and was appointed king over Israel.

David grew stronger and greater, for Jehovah the God of hosts was with him. And he reigned forty years over Israel as king.

10: KING SOLOMON

After the death of David, Solomon, his son, reigned in his stead. God endowed him with great wisdom, and added riches and honor to the length of his days.

Now there were two women, who had each borne a son. But one of the babes died, and his mother claimed the living child of her companion for her own. So they came to the king to settle the dispute. Solomon said, "Let the living child be divided, and each woman shall have a part." When the real mother heard that, she cried out and said, "Then let her have my son, but let him

not be slain." Then Solomon knew that she was the real mother, and ordered the child to be given to her unhurt.

And it came to pass in the fourth year of Solomon's reign that he began to build the house of Jehovah. It was built of stone made ready at the quarry, and there was neither hammer nor axe nor any tool of iron heard in the house while it was being built. And the whole house he overlaid with gold, until all the house was finished.

But King Solomon loved many foreign women and he had seven hundred wives and three hundred concubines. When Solomon was old, his wives turned his heart away from God, and his heart was not perfect with Jehovah as was the heart of his father David.

11: ELIJAH, THE PROPHET OF GOD

And it came to pass after the death of Solomon that many wicked kings ruled, and they caused the people of Israel to do evil.

In the days of the reign of the wicked king Ahab, there lived a prophet of the Lord named Elijah. And the word of the Lord came to Elijah to hide himself beside a brook. And the ravens brought him bread to eat in the morning and in the evening, and he drank from the brook.

God then told Elijah to challenge the four hundred and fifty prophets of Baal

to a contest at Mount Carmel. They would call upon their god and Elijah would call upon the name of the Lord. Elijah said to the people, "The God who answers by fire, let him be God."

From morning until evening the prophets of Baal called upon him to hear them. They cried aloud, and leaped upon the altar, and cut themselves with knives and lances. But there was no voice, nor any answer. And Elijah mocked them and said, "Cry louder. Either he is on a journey, or perhaps he is asleep and must be wakened." And the prophets cried out all the more.

Then Elijah had four jars of water poured on the altar with the sacrifice, not once but a second and third time. When Elijah had prayed, the fire of Jehovah fell and consumed the sacrifice, the wood and the stones, and licked up the water that was on the ground. When the people saw it, they fell on their faces and said, "Jehovah, he is God."

Elijah served the Lord faithfully until the end of his days. And there appeared a chariot of fire, and horses of fire, and Elijah went up by a whirlwind into heaven.

JONAH

On account of the great wickedness of the city of Nineveh, the Lord ordered the prophet Jonah to go and cry against it. But through fear, lack of faith, or some other cause, Jonah disobeyed the command of the Lord. And he went on a ship to run away to Tarshish.

But the Lord sent out a great wind, and there was a mighty tempest in the sea. When Jonah told the sailors of his disobedience, at his request they threw him overboard. A great fish, prepared

by the Lord, swallowed up Jonah and he was preserved in the belly for three days. Jonah repented and at the command of the Lord, the fish spit out Jonah onto the dry land. And Jonah went and preached to the people of Nineveh, who also repented and put their faith in Jehovah God.

DANIEL

In the court of Darius, a king of Persia, lived Daniel. He was a devout man and greatly favored by the king. Accordingly, the nobles envied Daniel and tried to destroy him. And they prevailed on the king to cast him

into a lions' den. But God, whom he served, closed their mouths and kept the lions from hurting him.

When Darius the king arose early in the morning and went to the den, he found Daniel alive and rejoiced greatly. He then caused those wicked men who had falsely accused Daniel to be thrown into the den, and the lions jumped on them, and broke their bones in pieces.

13: THE BIRTH OF CHRIST

About four thousand years after the fall of Adam by sin, God sent his only begotten Son, Jesus the Christ, the Savior, into the world. He was born in Bethlehem, a town of Judea, as had been foretold.

Now, as some shepherds watched their flocks at night, in the field, the angel of the Lord came upon them. A glorious light shone from heaven, and the angel said unto them, "Fear not; for behold I bring you good tidings of great joy, which shall be to all people. For unto you is born this day, in the city of David, a Savior, which is Christ the Lord. And this shall be a sign unto you: you shall find the babe wrapped in strips of cloth lying in a manger."

And suddenly there was with the angel a multitude of the heavenly host, praising God, and saying, "Glory to God in the highest, and on earth peace and goodwill toward men."

So, leaving their flocks, they went to Bethlehem where they found Mary, the mother of Jesus, and the babe lying in

a manger. Mary and Joseph had been journeying and there was no room for them in the inn. When the shepherds saw him, they worshipped, and were exceedingly glad.

There were also wise men in the east directed by a star, who sought the young child. They said, "Where is the one that is born king of the Jews?" And when they found him, they also worshipped him.

But Herod, the king, was exceedingly angry at this. He commanded that all the infants in Bethlehem, two years old and younger, should be slain. He hoped thereby to kill the infant Jesus.

14: FLIGHT INTO EGYPT

Then the angel of God appeared to Joseph, the husband of Mary, and said to him, "Arise and take the young child and his mother, and flee into Egypt. Stay there until I bring thee word, for Herod will seek the young child to destroy him."

So Joseph arose, and taking them by night, went as he was commanded. And they remained in Egypt until Herod died. Then the angel of the Lord appeared to him again, and told him to return with Jesus into his own land. For they that wished to take away his life were dead.

So they returned, and lived in Nazareth, fulfilling what was spoken by the prophet, that Jesus should be called a Nazarene.

And the child Jesus grew, and became strong in spirit. Filled with wisdom, the grace of God was upon him.

At a time when Jesus preached near the lake of Gennesaret, the multitude of those who came near him was so great, that he went into a ship nearby. And he taught them from the ship.

Afterwards, he said to Simon Peter, "Launch out into the deep, and let down your net." But Simon said, "Master, we have toiled all night, and have caught nothing. Nevertheless, at thy word I will let down the net."

So they did as Jesus commanded, and the net was so full of fish that it broke.

They beckoned partners for help, and they all greatly wondered.

Although Jesus went about doing good, the hearts of the people were hardened against him, and some secretly wished to destroy him.

So Nicodemus, who was a ruler among them, went to Jesus by night. He said, "We know that thou art a teacher come from God; for no man can do these miracles that thou doest, except God be with him."

Then Jesus informed him of the necessity of the new birth, and a change of heart and affections. And Jesus continued to teach him and said, "For God so

loved the world that he gave his only begotten Son, that whosoever believeth in him should not perish, but have eter- nal life."

16: JESUS WALKS ON THE WATER

Many wonderful things did Jesus do by word and deed. He caused the blind to see, the lame to walk, the deaf to hear, cleansed the lepers, raised the dead, and preached the gospel to the poor.

Having fed the five thousand, Jesus sent the disciples to go before him to the other side of the lake. But while the boat was in the middle of the sea, distressed by waves, Jesus came to them, walking on the water.

When the disciples saw him walking on the sea, they were troubled and cried out in fear, "It is a ghost." But Jesus spoke to them, saying, "Be of good cheer. It is I; be not afraid."

And Peter went down from the boat and walked upon the waters to Jesus. But when he saw the wind and the waves, he was afraid and began to sink. And those that were in the boat worshipped Jesus as the Son of God.

17: ACTS OF MINISTRY

Though Jesus possessed great wisdom and power, he was also a pattern of humility and compassion. For he loved to teach and comfort the poor and miserable.

Even little children he did not turn away, though his disciples would have sent them away. But Jesus said, "Let the little children come to me, and forbid them not, for such is the kingdom of heaven." Then he took them in his arms, and blessed them; and his blessing will remain upon all those who love and obey God.

As Jesus taught publicly, a certain man asked, "Who is my neighbor?" To which he replied, "A certain man fell among thieves, which stripped him, wounded him, and left him half dead. And by chance, there came down a priest and a Levite, and they looked on him and passed by on the other side.

"But a certain Samaritan walked by where he was. When he saw him, he had compassion for him. The Samaritan cleaned and bound up his wounds, pouring in oil and wine. Setting him on his own donkey, he brought him to an inn, and took care of him. He asked the innkeeper to care for him, promising to pay for all. Now, which of the three was

a neighbor to this man?" He said, "He that showed mercy to him." Then said Jesus, "Go, and do thou likewise."

Now a man named Lazarus, the brother of Mary and Martha, was sick. Therefore, his sisters sent word to Jesus to come and heal him.

When Jesus arrived in Bethany, Lazarus had already died and been in the tomb four days. Going to the tomb with Mary and Martha, who were weeping, Jesus was deeply moved in spirit. Seeing where they had laid him, Jesus wept.

Then Jesus called in a loud voice, "Lazarus, come out!" Suddenly, the

dead man came out of the tomb, his hands and feet wrapped in linen cloths. Jesus commanded, "Take off the grave clothes and let him go. He is alive!"

Jesus intended to go to Jerusalem and sent his disciples to find a young colt. As he rode toward the city, a great multitude spread their garments in the road. Others cut down branches from trees, and laid them in the road. And the multitudes that went before, and that followed, shouted, "Hosanna to the Son of David! Blessed is he that comes in the name of the Lord. Hosanna in the highest!"

Now, on the feast of the Passover, when Jesus and his disciples gathered to eat the Last Supper, they sat down together. And he said to them, "I have

desired to eat this Passover with you before I suffer." And he took bread, and gave thanks, and broke it and gave it to them. He said, "This is my body which is given for you. This do in remembrance of me." Likewise the cup, after supper saying, "This cup is the new testament in my blood, which is shed for you."

He then arose from supper, and laid aside his garments. Taking a towel and bowl of water, he washed his disciples' feet, and wiped them with the towel. Said Jesus, "If I, your Lord and Master, have washed your feet, you ought also to wash one another's feet." This was one more clear example, indeed, of humility and loving kindness.

19: TRIAL AND CRUCIFIXION

After this time, Judas was bribed by the Jews and agreed to betray Jesus into their hands. So a great multitude came out armed to take him. And Judas, with pretended kindness, went up and kissed him. This was the sign agreed upon, that the Jews might know which was the man they sought.

Then they laid hands on him, and led him away to Pontius Pilate, the governor. And his accusers began to bring many false charges against him. But Jesus, aware of his own innocence, answered nothing to all their accusations.

Pilate, perceiving they were only moved by envy and malice, said, "I see nothing in this man worthy of death. What then shall I do unto him?" And they all vehemently cried out, "Let him be crucified." Pilate again asked, "Why, what evil has he done?" Then they only exclaimed so much the more, "Crucify him! Crucify him!"

Pilate then took water and washed his hands, saying, "I am innocent of the blood of this just person. See ye to it." The soldiers then led Jesus into the common hall, where they treated him with terrible cruelty and insult. Having clothed him in scarlet, and put a crown made of thorns upon his head, they kneeled down in derision. Bowing in contempt before him, they hailed him King of the Jews. Some spit upon him, and others scourged him.

To all this, he never returned one angry word. But when nailed to the cross on Mount Calvary, he prayed for them, saying, "Father, forgive them; they know not what they do." In this way he left a bright and shining example of the precepts he had so often taught.

20: RESURRECTION AND ASCENSION

After Jesus had died, Joseph of Arimathea, an honorable counselor and disciple of Jesus, begged for the body. He laid it in a new tomb which had been cut out of a rock. This tomb had never been used.

On the third day, Jesus arose from the dead, showing himself alive to many people. First, he was seen by Mary Magdalene, and other devout women; then by Peter and John; then by the eleven; and after that, by about five hundred brethren at once.

on which Christ arose, being
st day of the week, was celebrat-
nstead of the Jewish Sabbath, to
kept holy. This they did in remem-
rance of his resurrection, and of our
redemption by him.

Our Lord ratified the powers given before to his apostles and invested them
with the same commission his Father
had given him. Said Jesus, "As my
Father has sent me, even so I send you."

Having spoken to his apostles of the
things pertaining to the kingdom of
God for forty days, Jesus commanded
them that they should be witnesses to
the uttermost parts of the earth. While

he blessed them, a cloud
out of their sight, and he
heaven.

The day
he fir
d